I0621995

# Meditating on the Glorious Mysteries

## An Intentional Rosary

## Amy Schisler

Bozman, MD 2023

ISBN: 979-8-9883677-7-2

Published by:
Chesapeake Sunrise Publishing
Amy Schisler
Bozman, MD
2023

# $T$able of Contents

# $\mathcal{H}$ow to use this book

An intentional Rosary is said with a pause before each Hail Mary within the five decades of the Rosary. This pause enables you to insert your own petition or to pray for the needs or prayer requests of others. The petitions in this book are inserted so you may meditate more deeply on the Glorious Mysteries. You may follow the prayers included, or you may substitute your own prayers. A favorite prayer of mine is The Memorare. I always close my Rosary with this prayer. I have included it at the end of the Rosary for your use.

May our Blessed Mother and her Son bestow upon you many blessings as you follow her request to pray the Rosary.

From the United States Conference of Catholic Bishops:
*The Rosary is a Scripture-based prayer. It begins with the Apostles' Creed, which summarizes the great mysteries of the Catholic faith. The Our*

*Father, which introduces each mystery, is from the Gospels. The first part of the Hail Mary is the angel's words announcing Christ's birth and Elizabeth's greeting to Mary. St. Pius V officially added the second part of the Hail Mary. The Mysteries of the Rosary center on the events of Christ's life. There are four sets of Mysteries: Glorious , Sorrowful, Glorious and—added by Saint John Paul II in 2002—the Luminous.*

Typical Days to Pray Each Rosary:
Sunday and Wednesday – Glorious
Monday and Saturday – Joyful
Tuesday and Friday – Sorrowful
Thursday – Luminous

# *T*he Beginning of the Rosary

In the Name of the Father, and of the
Son, and of the Holy Spirit. Amen

I believe in God,
the Father almighty,
Creator of heaven and earth,
and in Jesus Christ, his only Son, our
Lord,
who was conceived by the Holy Spirit,
born of the Virgin Mary,
suffered under Pontius Pilate,
was crucified, died and was buried;
he descended into hell;
on the third day he rose again from the
dead;
he ascended into heaven,
and is seated at the right hand of God the
Father almighty;
from there he will come to judge the
living and the dead.
I believe in the Holy Spirit,
the holy catholic Church,
the communion of saints,
the forgiveness of sins,

the resurrection of the body,
and life everlasting.
Amen.


Our Father, who art in Heaven, hallowed
be thy name.
Thy kingdom come.
Thy will be done on Earth as it is in
Heaven.
Give us this day our daily bread,
And forgive us our trespasses as we
forgive those who trespass against us.
And lead us not into temptation, but
deliver us from evil.
Amen


For the grace of Faith:
Hail Mary, full of grace.
The Lord is with thee.
Blessed art thou among women,
And blessed is the fruit of thy womb,
Jesus.
Holy Mary, Mother of God,
Pray for us sinners,
Now and at the hour of death.
Amen
For the grace of Hope:

Hail Mary, full of grace.
The Lord is with thee.
Blessed art thou among women,
And blessed is the fruit of thy womb,
Jesus.
Holy Mary, Mother of God,
Pray for us sinners,
Now and at the hour of death.
Amen

For the grace of Charity:
Hail Mary, full of grace.
The Lord is with thee.
Blessed art thou among women,
And blessed is the fruit of thy womb,
Jesus.
Holy Mary, Mother of God,
Pray for us sinners,
Now and at the hour of death.
Amen

Glory be to the Father,
And the Son,
And the Holy Spirit,
As now and ever shall be,
World without end.
Amen

# *T*he First Glorious Mystery:

## The Resurrection
Matthew 28:1-10

*After the sabbath, as the first day of the week was dawning, Mary Magdalene and the other Mary came to see the tomb. And behold, there was a great earthquake; for an angel of the Lord descended from heaven, approached, rolled back the stone, and sat upon it. His appearance was like lightning and his clothing was white as snow. The guards were shaken with fear of him and became like dead men.*

*Then the angel said to the women in reply, "Do not be afraid! I know that you are seeking Jesus the crucified. He is not here, for he has been raised just as he said. Come and see the place where he lay. Then go quickly and tell his disciples, 'He has been raised from the dead, and he is going before you to Galilee; there you will see him.' Behold, I have told you."*

*Then they went away quickly from the tomb, fearful yet overjoyed, and ran to announce this to his disciples. And behold, Jesus met them on their way and greeted them. They approached, embraced his feet, and did him homage. Then Jesus said to them, "Do not be afraid. Go tell my brothers to go to Galilee, and there they will see me."*

Our Father, who art in Heaven, hallowed be thy name.
Thy kingdom come.
Thy will be done on Earth as it is in Heaven.
Give us this day our daily bread,
And forgive us our trespasses as we forgive those who trespass against us.
And lead us not into temptation, but deliver us from evil.
Amen

*For the repose of the souls of our family members who await the resurrection of their bodies:*
Hail Mary, full of grace.
The Lord is with thee.
Blessed art thou among women,
And blessed is the fruit of thy womb, Jesus.
Holy Mary, Mother of God,
Pray for us sinners,

Now and at the hour of death.
Amen

*For the souls in purgatory who are being purified
so they may see God in His glory:*
Hail Mary, full of grace.
The Lord is with thee.
Blessed art thou among women,
And blessed is the fruit of thy womb,
Jesus.
Holy Mary, Mother of God,
Pray for us sinners,
Now and at the hour of death.
Amen

*For those who have gone to their eternal rest
without knowing God:*
Hail Mary, full of grace.
The Lord is with thee.
Blessed art thou among women,
And blessed is the fruit of thy womb,
Jesus.
Holy Mary, Mother of God,
Pray for us sinners,
Now and at the hour of death.
Amen
*For those who will soon leave this earth with the*

*hope of rising again:*
Hail Mary, full of grace.
The Lord is with thee.
Blessed art thou among women,
And blessed is the fruit of thy womb,
Jesus.
Holy Mary, Mother of God,
Pray for us sinners,
Now and at the hour of death.
Amen

*For the families who mourn the dearly departed:*
Hail Mary, full of grace.
The Lord is with thee.
Blessed art thou among women,
And blessed is the fruit of thy womb,
Jesus.
Holy Mary, Mother of God,
Pray for us sinners,
Now and at the hour of death.
Amen

*For the men and women who take care of the
dead in funeral homes and cemeteries:*
Hail Mary, full of grace.
The Lord is with thee.
Blessed art thou among women,

And blessed is the fruit of thy womb,
Jesus.
Holy Mary, Mother of God,
Pray for us sinners,
Now and at the hour of death.
Amen

*For those facing a new way of life after the loss
of a loved one:*
Hail Mary, full of grace.
The Lord is with thee.
Blessed art thou among women,
And blessed is the fruit of thy womb,
Jesus.
Holy Mary, Mother of God,
Pray for us sinners,
Now and at the hour of death.
Amen

*For the courage to take God's Word back to our
friends and families:*
Hail Mary, full of grace.
The Lord is with thee.
Blessed art thou among women,
And blessed is the fruit of thy womb,
Jesus.
Holy Mary, Mother of God,
Pray for us sinners,

Now and at the hour of death.
Amen

*For teachers and catechists who teach the Good
News to the faithful:*
Hail Mary, full of grace.
The Lord is with thee.
Blessed art thou among women,
And blessed is the fruit of thy womb,
Jesus.
Holy Mary, Mother of God,
Pray for us sinners,
Now and at the hour of death.
Amen

*For the health and safety of missionaries
everywhere, working to spread the Good News:*
Hail Mary, full of grace.
The Lord is with thee.
Blessed art thou among women,
And blessed is the fruit of thy womb,
Jesus.
Holy Mary, Mother of God,
Pray for us sinners,
Now and at the hour of death.
Amen
Glory be to the Father,

And the Son,
And the Holy Spirit,
As now and ever shall be,
World without end.
Amen

O my Jesus, forgive us our sins, save us
from the fires of hell; lead all souls to
Heaven, especially those who have most
need of your mercy.

# *T*he Second Glorious Mystery:

## The Ascension of our Lord into Heaven
Acts 1:6-11

*When they had gathered together they asked him, "Lord, are you at this time going to restore the kingdom to Israel?" He answered them, "It is not for you to know the times or seasons that the Father has established by his own authority. But you will receive power when the holy Spirit comes upon you, and you will be my witnesses in Jerusalem, throughout Judea and Samaria, and to the ends of the earth."*

*When he had said this, as they were looking on, he was lifted up, and a cloud took him from their sight. While they were looking intently at the sky as he was going, suddenly two men dressed in white garments stood beside them. They said, "Men of Galilee, why are you standing there looking at the sky? This Jesus who has been taken up from you into heaven will return in the same way as you have seen him going into heaven."*

Our Father, who art in Heaven, hallowed
be thy name.
Thy kingdom come.
Thy will be done on Earth as it is in
Heaven.
Give us this day our daily bread,
And forgive us our trespasses as we
forgive those who trespass against us.
And lead us not into temptation, but
deliver us from evil.
Amen

*For all the faithful awaiting the return of the
Lord:*
Hail Mary, full of grace.
The Lord is with thee.
Blessed art thou among women,
And blessed is the fruit of thy womb,
Jesus.
Holy Mary, Mother of God,
Pray for us sinners,
Now and at the hour of death.
Amen

*For our Jewish brothers and sisters awaiting the
restoration of the kingdom:*
Hail Mary, full of grace.

The Lord is with thee.
Blessed art thou among women,
And blessed is the fruit of thy womb,
Jesus.
Holy Mary, Mother of God,
Pray for us sinners,
Now and at the hour of death.
Amen

*For peace in Jerusalem, Judea, Samaria, Galilee, and all the Holy Land:*
Hail Mary, full of grace.
The Lord is with thee.
Blessed art thou among women,
And blessed is the fruit of thy womb,
Jesus.
Holy Mary, Mother of God,
Pray for us sinners,
Now and at the hour of death.
Amen

*For those who give witness to the power of God in their lives:*
Hail Mary, full of grace.
The Lord is with thee.
Blessed art thou among women,
And blessed is the fruit of thy womb,

Jesus.
Holy Mary, Mother of God,
Pray for us sinners,
Now and at the hour of death.
Amen

*For priests and bishops who take the Lord's*
*message to the ends of the earth:*
Hail Mary, full of grace.
The Lord is with thee.
Blessed art thou among women,
And blessed is the fruit of thy womb,
Jesus.
Holy Mary, Mother of God,
Pray for us sinners,
Now and at the hour of death.
Amen

*That the Word of God reaches the entire world:*
Hail Mary, full of grace.
The Lord is with thee.
Blessed art thou among women,
And blessed is the fruit of thy womb,
Jesus.
Holy Mary, Mother of God,
Pray for us sinners,
Now and at the hour of death.

Amen

*For those who are still looking for the Lord:*
Hail Mary, full of grace.
The Lord is with thee.
Blessed art thou among women,
And blessed is the fruit of thy womb,
Jesus.
Holy Mary, Mother of God,
Pray for us sinners,
Now and at the hour of death.
Amen

*For our protection by our guardian angels:*
Hail Mary, full of grace.
The Lord is with thee.
Blessed art thou among women,
And blessed is the fruit of thy womb,
Jesus.
Holy Mary, Mother of God,
Pray for us sinners,
Now and at the hour of death.
Amen

*For those looking forward to being reunited with loved ones:*
Hail Mary, full of grace.

The Lord is with thee.
Blessed art thou among women,
And blessed is the fruit of thy womb,
Jesus.
Holy Mary, Mother of God,
Pray for us sinners,
Now and at the hour of death.
Amen

*For the wisdom and courage to follow the path
God has laid out for me for my life:*
Hail Mary, full of grace.
The Lord is with thee.
Blessed art thou among women,
And blessed is the fruit of thy womb,
Jesus.
Holy Mary, Mother of God,
Pray for us sinners,
Now and at the hour of death.
Amen

Glory be to the Father,
And the Son,
And the Holy Spirit,
As now and ever shall be,
World without end.
Amen

O my Jesus, forgive us our sins, save us from the fires of hell; lead all souls to Heaven, especially those who have most need of your mercy.

# *T*he Third Glorious Mystery:

## The Descent of the Holy Spirit at Pentecost
Acts 2:1-8,11

*When the time for Pentecost was fulfilled, they were all in one place together. And suddenly there came from the sky a noise like a strong driving wind, and it filled the entire house in which they were. Then there appeared to them tongues as of fire, which parted and came to rest on each one of them. And they were all filled with the holy Spirit and began to speak in different tongues, as the Spirit enabled them to proclaim.*

*Now there were devout Jews from every nation under heaven staying in Jerusalem. At this sound, they gathered in a large crowd, but they were confused because each one heard them speaking in his own language. They were astounded, and in amazement they asked, "Are not all these people who are speaking Galileans? Then how does each of us hear them...speaking in our own tongues of the mighty acts of God."*

Our Father, who art in Heaven, hallowed
be thy name.
Thy kingdom come.
Thy will be done on Earth as it is in
Heaven.
Give us this day our daily bread,
And forgive us our trespasses as we
forgive those who trespass against us.
And lead us not into temptation, but
deliver us from evil.
Amen

*For Confirmandi preparing for the Sacrament of
Confirmation:*
Hail Mary, full of grace.
The Lord is with thee.
Blessed art thou among women,
And blessed is the fruit of thy womb,
Jesus.
Holy Mary, Mother of God,
Pray for us sinners,
Now and at the hour of death.
Amen

*For Confirmation sponsors guiding others to the
Holy Spirit:*
Hail Mary, full of grace.

The Lord is with thee.
Blessed art thou among women,
And blessed is the fruit of thy womb,
Jesus.
Holy Mary, Mother of God,
Pray for us sinners,
Now and at the hour of death.
Amen

*For all those who teach others about The Father,
the Son, and the Holy Spirit:*
Hail Mary, full of grace.
The Lord is with thee.
Blessed art thou among women,
And blessed is the fruit of thy womb,
Jesus.
Holy Mary, Mother of God,
Pray for us sinners,
Now and at the hour of death.
Amen

*For those in hiding—mentally, spiritually, or
physically—in fear:*
Hail Mary, full of grace.
The Lord is with thee.
Blessed art thou among women,
And blessed is the fruit of thy womb,

Jesus.
Holy Mary, Mother of God,
Pray for us sinners,
Now and at the hour of death.
Amen

*For those trying to speak to others in foreign
lands about the works of God:*
Hail Mary, full of grace.
The Lord is with thee.
Blessed art thou among women,
And blessed is the fruit of thy womb,
Jesus.
Holy Mary, Mother of God,
Pray for us sinners,
Now and at the hour of death.
Amen

*For those who are confused by God's message to
them:*
Hail Mary, full of grace.
The Lord is with thee.
Blessed art thou among women,
And blessed is the fruit of thy womb,
Jesus.
Holy Mary, Mother of God,
Pray for us sinners,

Now and at the hour of death.
Amen

*For clarity in my own mission:*
Hail Mary, full of grace.
The Lord is with thee.
Blessed art thou among women,
And blessed is the fruit of thy womb,
Jesus.
Holy Mary, Mother of God,
Pray for us sinners,
Now and at the hour of death.
Amen

*For clarity for my loved ones who are seeking
God and His purpose for them:*
Hail Mary, full of grace.
The Lord is with thee.
Blessed art thou among women,
And blessed is the fruit of thy womb,
Jesus.
Holy Mary, Mother of God,
Pray for us sinners,
Now and at the hour of death.
Amen
*For the devout who are trying to live faithfully in
our fallen world:*

Hail Mary, full of grace.
The Lord is with thee.
Blessed art thou among women,
And blessed is the fruit of thy womb,
Jesus.
Holy Mary, Mother of God,
Pray for us sinners,
Now and at the hour of death.
Amen

*For those listening for the voice of God.*
Hail Mary, full of grace.
The Lord is with thee.
Blessed art thou among women,
And blessed is the fruit of thy womb,
Jesus.
Holy Mary, Mother of God,
Pray for us sinners,
Now and at the hour of death.
Amen

Glory be to the Father,
And the Son,
And the Holy Spirit,
As now and ever shall be,
World without end.
Amen

O my Jesus, forgive us our sins, save us from the fires of hell; lead all souls to Heaven, especially those who have most need of your mercy.

# *T*he Fourth Glorious Mystery:
## The Assumption of Mary
CCC 965

*Finally the Immaculate Virgin, preserved free from all stain of original sin, when the course of her earthly life was finished, was taken up body and soul into heavenly glory, and exalted by the Lord as Queen over all things, so that she might be the more fully conformed to her Son, the Lord of lords and conqueror of sin and death." The Assumption of the Blessed Virgin is a singular participation in her Son's Resurrection and an anticipation of the resurrection of other Christians:*

*In giving birth you kept your virginity; in your Dormition* [eternal sleep] *you did not leave the world, O Mother of God, but were joined to the source of Life. You conceived the living God and, by your prayers, will deliver our souls from death.*

Our Father, who art in Heaven, hallowed be thy name.
Thy kingdom come.
Thy will be done on Earth as it is in

Heaven.

Give us this day our daily bread,

And forgive us our trespasses as we forgive those who trespass against us.

And lead us not into temptation, but deliver us from evil.

Amen

*That I will use all my gifts and talents to glorify the Lord:*

Hail Mary, full of grace.

The Lord is with thee.

Blessed art thou among women,

And blessed is the fruit of thy womb, Jesus.

Holy Mary, Mother of God,

Pray for us sinners,

Now and at the hour of death.

Amen

*For those who are unable to find peace in their bodies, that they will turn to the Lord for help and guidance:*

Hail Mary, full of grace.

The Lord is with thee.

Blessed art thou among women,

And blessed is the fruit of thy womb, Jesus.

Holy Mary, Mother of God,
Pray for us sinners,
Now and at the hour of death.
Amen

*For those who do harm to their own bodies, that
they will see their bodies as temples of the Lord:*
Hail Mary, full of grace.
The Lord is with thee.
Blessed art thou among women,
And blessed is the fruit of thy womb,
Jesus.
Holy Mary, Mother of God,
Pray for us sinners,
Now and at the hour of death.
Amen

*For those whose bodies lead them into sin, may
they seek God's grace:*
Hail Mary, full of grace.
The Lord is with thee.
Blessed art thou among women,
And blessed is the fruit of thy womb,
Jesus.
Holy Mary, Mother of God,
Pray for us sinners,
Now and at the hour of death.

Amen

*For young people to see the beauty in chastity:*
Hail Mary, full of grace.
The Lord is with thee.
Blessed art thou among women,
And blessed is the fruit of thy womb,
Jesus.
Holy Mary, Mother of God,
Pray for us sinners,
Now and at the hour of death.
Amen

*For married couples to understand how to seek chastity in marriage by giving to each other in faith, trust, and complete love:*
Hail Mary, full of grace.
The Lord is with thee.
Blessed art thou among women,
And blessed is the fruit of thy womb,
Jesus.
Holy Mary, Mother of God,
Pray for us sinners,
Now and at the hour of death.
Amen
*For family and friends struggling with sins of the flesh:*

Hail Mary, full of grace.
The Lord is with thee.
Blessed art thou among women,
And blessed is the fruit of thy womb,
Jesus.
Holy Mary, Mother of God,
Pray for us sinners,
Now and at the hour of death.
Amen

*For the intercession of Mary in Heaven for my*
*children and those who are like children to me:*
Hail Mary, full of grace.
The Lord is with thee.
Blessed art thou among women,
And blessed is the fruit of thy womb,
Jesus.
Holy Mary, Mother of God,
Pray for us sinners,
Now and at the hour of death.
Amen

*For those whose bodies are failing them:*
Hail Mary, full of grace.
The Lord is with thee.
Blessed art thou among women,
And blessed is the fruit of thy womb,

Jesus.
Holy Mary, Mother of God,
Pray for us sinners,
Now and at the hour of death.
Amen

*That my soul will be delivered from death:*
Hail Mary, full of grace.
The Lord is with thee.
Blessed art thou among women,
And blessed is the fruit of thy womb,
Jesus.
Holy Mary, Mother of God,
Pray for us sinners,
Now and at the hour of death.
Amen

Glory be to the Father,
And the Son,
And the Holy Spirit,
As now and ever shall be,
World without end.
Amen

O my Jesus, forgive us our sins, save us
from the fires of hell; lead all souls to
Heaven, especially those who have most

need of your mercy.

# *T*he Fifth Glorious Mystery: The Coronation of Mary as Queen of Heaven
Revelation 12:1

*A great sign appeared in the sky, a woman clothed with the sun, with the moon under her feet, and on her head a crown of twelve stars.*

Our Father, who art in Heaven, hallowed be thy name.
Thy kingdom come.
Thy will be done on Earth as it is in Heaven.
Give us this day our daily bread,
And forgive us our trespasses as we forgive those who trespass against us.
And lead us not into temptation, but deliver us from evil.
Amen

*For the Church, our Mother on Earth:*
Hail Mary, full of grace.
The Lord is with thee.
Blessed art thou among women,

And blessed is the fruit of thy womb,
Jesus.
Holy Mary, Mother of God,
Pray for us sinners,
Now and at the hour of death.
Amen

*For our earthly mothers, living and deceased:*
Hail Mary, full of grace.
The Lord is with thee.
Blessed art thou among women,
And blessed is the fruit of thy womb,
Jesus.
Holy Mary, Mother of God,
Pray for us sinners,
Now and at the hour of death.
Amen

*That mothers will have wisdom, patience, and
unfailing love in raising their children:*
Hail Mary, full of grace.
The Lord is with thee.
Blessed art thou among women,
And blessed is the fruit of thy womb,
Jesus.
Holy Mary, Mother of God,
Pray for us sinners,

Now and at the hour of death.
Amen

*For wisdom in my role as a mother or mother-figure:*
Hail Mary, full of grace.
The Lord is with thee.
Blessed art thou among women,
And blessed is the fruit of thy womb,
Jesus.
Holy Mary, Mother of God,
Pray for us sinners,
Now and at the hour of death.
Amen

*For the ability to be an intercessor for those in need:*
Hail Mary, full of grace.
The Lord is with thee.
Blessed art thou among women,
And blessed is the fruit of thy womb,
Jesus.
Holy Mary, Mother of God,
Pray for us sinners,
Now and at the hour of death.
Amen
*For all women seeking a more intimate*

*relationship with Jesus and His Mother:*
Hail Mary, full of grace.
The Lord is with thee.
Blessed art thou among women,
And blessed is the fruit of thy womb,
Jesus.
Holy Mary, Mother of God,
Pray for us sinners,
Now and at the hour of death.
Amen

*That I may imitate Mary's devotion to her Son:*
Hail Mary, full of grace.
The Lord is with thee.
Blessed art thou among women,
And blessed is the fruit of thy womb,
Jesus.
Holy Mary, Mother of God,
Pray for us sinners,
Now and at the hour of death.
Amen

*That I may be a spiritual mother to those in need:*
Hail Mary, full of grace.
The Lord is with thee.
Blessed art thou among women,

And blessed is the fruit of thy womb,
Jesus.
Holy Mary, Mother of God,
Pray for us sinners,
Now and at the hour of death.
Amen

*That, like Mary, I may be a model of faith and
charity:*
Hail Mary, full of grace.
The Lord is with thee.
Blessed art thou among women,
And blessed is the fruit of thy womb,
Jesus.
Holy Mary, Mother of God,
Pray for us sinners,
Now and at the hour of death.
Amen

*That, like Mary, I may cooperate with and aid
Jesus in His work on Earth:*
Hail Mary, full of grace.
The Lord is with thee.
Blessed art thou among women,
And blessed is the fruit of thy womb,
Jesus.
Holy Mary, Mother of God,

Pray for us sinners,
Now and at the hour of death.
Amen

Glory be to the Father,
And the Son,
And the Holy Spirit,
As now and ever shall be,
World without end.
Amen

O my Jesus, forgive us our sins, save us
from the fires of hell; lead all souls to
Heaven, especially those who have most
need of your mercy.

# *T*he End of the Rosary

Hail, Holy Queen, Mother of Mercy,
our life, our sweetness and our hope.
To thee do we cry,
poor banished children of Eve.
To thee do we send up our sighs,
mourning and weeping in this valley of
tears.
Turn then, most gracious advocate,
thine eyes of mercy toward us,
and after this our exile
show unto us the blessed fruit of thy
womb, Jesus.
O clement, O loving,
O sweet Virgin Mary.

Pray for us, O holy Mother of God.
That we may be made worthy of the
promises of Christ

O God, whose Only Begotten Son, by
his life, Death, and Resurrection, has
purchased for us the rewards of eternal
life, grant, we beseech thee, that while
meditating on these mysteries of the

most holy Rosary of the Blessed Virgin Mary, we may imitate what they contain and obtain what they promise, through the same Christ our Lord. Amen.

# The Memorare

Remember, O most gracious Virgin Mary, that never was it known that anyone who fled to thy protection, implored thy help, or sought thy intercession, was left unaided.

Inspired by this confidence I fly unto thee, O Virgin of virgins, my Mother.

To thee do I come, before thee I stand, sinful and sorrowful.

O Mother of the Word Incarnate, despise not my petitions, but in thy mercy hear and answer me.

Amen.


In the Name of the Father, and of the Son, and of the Holy Spirit.

Amen

# *P*rayers and Petitions

---

---

---

---

---

---

---

---

---